To

From

Words to Warm a Mother's Heart
© 2008 Summerside Press
www.summersidepress.com

Cover & Interior Design by
Müllerhaus Publishing Group | www.mullerhaus.net

Scripture references are from the following sources: The Holy Bible,
New International Version® NIV®. © 1973, 1978, 1984 by International
Bible Society. Used by permission of Zondervan. The New King James
Version (NKJV). Copyright © 1982 by Thomas Nelson, Inc. Used by
permission. The Holy Bible, New Living Translation® (NLT). Copyright
© 1996, 2004. Used by permission of Tyndale House Publishers, Inc.,
Wheaton, Illinois. The Message © 1993, 1994, 1995, 1996, 2000, 2001,
2002 by Eugene Peterson. Used by permission of NavPress, Colorado
Springs, CO. The New Century Version® (NCV). Copyright © 1987,
1988, 1991 by Thomas Nelson, Inc. Used by permission. All rights
reserved.

Excluding Scripture verses, references to men and masculine pronouns
have been replaced with gender-neutral references.

ISBN 978-1-934770-42-9

Printed in China

WORDS TO WARM

· · · A · · ·

Mother's
HEART

summerside
PRESS

TABLE OF CONTENTS

• • • • • • • • • • • • • • • • • • • •

WISDOM TO LIVE BY	5
THE BEAUTY OF LIFE	11
LIVING IN TRUTH	17
GOD BLESS YOU	23
THE GIFT OF SIMPLICITY	29
MY HEART IS CONTENT	35
PROVIDING ALL OUR NEEDS	41
BE ENCOURAGED	47
TAKING TIME TO LOVE	53
I BELIEVE	59
A COVERING OF PRAYER	65
THE STRENGTH OF FAMILY	71
THANK YOU, LORD!	77
THE RICHNESS OF FRIENDSHIP	83
LOVE ALL AROUND	89
SPECIAL GIFTS WE SHARE	95
TO LIVE, LAUGH, AND LOVE	101
GOD OUR FATHER	107
HEART FULL OF JOY	113
A MOTHER'S INFLUENCE	119
GRATITUDE	125

Wisdom
to Live By

All things bright and beautiful,
All creatures great and small,
All things wise and wonderful,
The Lord God made them all.

CECIL FRANCES ALEXANDER

*The wise don't expect
to find life worth living;
they make it that way.*

Those who came before us will teach you.
They will teach you the wisdom of old.

JOB 8:10 NLT

Heavenly Father,
please give me wisdom
in daily protecting my children.
Whether it's concerning
the people they come in contact with,
the television and videos they watch,
or the many other issues that affect them,
may I be aware of my responsibility
to guide and nurture their minds.
Amen.

KIM BOYCE

I am convinced
beyond a shadow of any doubt
that the most valuable pursuit
we can embark upon
is to know God.

KAY ARTHUR

Wisdom is knowing the truth,
and telling it.

Having three children in three years
was a great pruning
experience in my life.
It was God's creative way
of putting me in a situation
where I had to learn patience.

CYNTHIA HEALD

7

At the end of your life
you will never regret
not having passed one more test,
not winning one more verdict,
or not closing one more deal.
You will regret time not spent
with a husband, a friend,
a child, or a parent.

BARBARA BUSH

Wonder is
the beginning of wisdom.

Whenever I need help being a mother,
I remember my mother and grandmother,
women who planted seeds of wisdom in my soul,
like a secret garden,
to flower even in the bitterest cold.

JUDITH TOWSE-ROBERTS

True wisdom and power
are found in God;
counsel and understanding
are His.

JOB 12:13 NLT

*A child's hand in yours—
what tenderness
and power it arouses.
You are instantly
the very touchstone
of wisdom and strength.*

MARJORIE HOLMES

We ought to be able to learn things secondhand.
There is not enough time for us
to make all the mistakes ourselves.

HARRIET HALL

A wise gardener plants his seeds,
then has the good sense not to dig them up
every few days to see if a crop is on the way.
Likewise, we must be patient
as God brings the answers...
in His own good time.

QUIN SHERRER

For the wisdom of the
wisest being God has made
ends in wonder;
and there is nothing on earth
so wonderful as
the budding soul of a little child.

LUCY LARCOM

The Beauty of Life

To be a child is to know the joy of living.
To have a child is to know the beauty of life.

As God's workmanship, we deserve to be treated, and to
treat ourselves, with affection and affirmation,
regardless of our appearance or performance.

MARY ANN MAYO

*Something deep in all of us yearns
for God's beauty, and we can find it
no matter where we are.*

SUE MONK KIDD

Most of all the other beautiful things in life come by twos
and threes, by dozens and hundreds. Plenty of roses,
stars, sunsets, rainbows, brothers and sisters, aunts and
cousins, comrades and friends—but only one mother
in the whole world.

KATE DOUGLAS WIGGIN

You are God's created beauty and the focus of
His affection and delight.

JANET WEAVER SMITH

We are so busy in our lives that we need to
purposely give attention to the everyday things
that can make our lives lovelier, such as
keeping a vase of fresh flowers in an obvious place,
or several places in the house.
Planting roses or other flowers for
this purpose makes sense.

EMILIE BARNES

Therefore, as God's chosen people, holy and dearly loved,
clothe yourselves with compassion, kindness, humility,
gentleness and patience.

COLOSSIANS 3:12 NIV

Today a new sun rises for me; everything lives, everything
is animated, everything seems to speak to me of my
passion, everything invites me to cherish it.

ANNE DE LENCLOS

Consider the lilies, how they grow: they neither toil
nor spin; and yet I say to you, even Solomon in all his
glory was not arrayed like one of these. If then God so
clothes the grass, which today is in the field and
tomorrow is thrown into the oven,
how much more will He clothe you?

LUKE 12:27-28 NKJV

For attractive lips,
Speak words of kindness.
For lovely eyes,
Seek out the good in people.
For a slim figure,
Share your food with the hungry.
For beautiful hair,
Let a child run his or her fingers through it once a day.
For poise,
Walk with the knowledge you'll never walk alone.

AUDREY HEPBURN

Beauty puts a face on God. When we gaze at nature, at a loved one, at a work of art, our soul immediately recognizes and is drawn to the face of God.

MARGARET BROWNLEY

May God give you eyes to see beauty only the heart can understand.

Every time you smile at someone, it is an action of love, a gift to that person, a beautiful thing.

MOTHER TERESA

The Lord is all I need. He takes care of me. My share in life has been pleasant; my part has been beautiful.

PSALM 16:5-6 NCV

Isn't it a wonderful morning?
The world looks like something
God had just imagined for His own pleasure.

LUCY MAUD MONTGOMERY

Let there be many windows in your soul,
That all the glory of the universe may beautify it.

ELLA WHEELER WILCOX

Ask any four-year-old boy,
"Who's the most beautiful woman in the world?"
His mommy! Ask any grown daughter
caring for her aging mother the same question,
and you'll get the same answer....
Moms spend a lifetime humbling themselves
in taking care of others. Nothing is more attractive.

LISA WHELCHEL

In all ranks of life the human heart yearns for the
beautiful, and the beautiful things that God
makes are His gift to all alike.

HARRIET BEECHER STOWE

Living in Truth

Truth...has got to be concrete.
And there's nothing more concrete than dealing with
babies, burps, bottles and frogs.

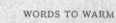
Truth is always exciting.
Speak it, then.
Life is dull without it.
PEARL S. BUCK

Anyone who examines this evidence
will come to stake his life on this:
that God Himself is the truth.
JOHN 3:31 THE MESSAGE

Amid ancient lore
the Word of God stands unique and pre-eminent.
Wonderful in its construction,
admirable in its adaptation,
it contains truths
that a child may comprehend,
and mysteries into which
angels desire to look.
FRANCES ELLEN WATKINS HARPER

To follow truth as blind men long for light,
To do my best from dawn of day till night,
To keep my heart fit for His holy sight,
And answer when He calls.
This is my task.

MAUDE LOUISE RAY

*Jesus answered,
"I am the way and the truth and the life.
No one comes to the Father
except through Me."*

JOHN 14:6 NIV

Truth-tellers are not always palatable. There is a
preference for candy bars.

GWENDOLYN BROOKS

19

Open my eyes that I may see
Glimpses of truth Thou hast for me.
Place in my hands the wonderful key
That shall unclasp and set me free:
Silently now I wait for Thee,
Ready, my God, Thy will to see;
Open my eyes, illumine me,
Spirit divine!

CLARA H. SCOTT

I am amazed by the sayings of Christ.
They seem truer than anything
I have ever read.
And they certainly turn the world
upside down.

KATHERINE BUTLER HATHAWAY

We live in the present,
we dream of the future,
but we learn eternal truths
from the past.

LUCY MAUD MONTGOMERY

Every good action and
every perfect gift is from God.
These good gifts come down
from the Creator of the sun, moon, and stars,
who does not change
like their shifting shadows.
God decided to give us life
through the word of truth
so we might be the most important
of all the things He made.

JAMES 1:17-18 NCV

It is an extraordinary
and beautiful thing
that God, in creation...
works with the beauty of matter;
the reality of things;
the discoveries of the senses,
all five of them;
so that we, in turn,
may hear the grass growing;
see a face springing to life
in love and laughter....
The offerings of creation...
our glimpses of truth.

Madeleine L'Engle

God Bless You

A mother is a gift from God
that's blessed in every part...
born through love and loyalty...
conceived within the heart.

I will let God's peace infuse every part of today. As the
chaos swirls and life's demands pull at me on all sides,
I will breathe in God's peace that surpasses
all understanding. He has promised that He would set
within me a peace too deeply planted to be affected by
unexpected or exhausting demands.

Parents who instruct and nurture their children in God's
ways will see fulfilled that great promise—
"he will not depart from it."

CATHERINE MARSHALL

Children, obey your parents in the Lord, for this is right.
"Honor your father and mother," which is the first
commandment with promise: "that it may be well with
you and you may live long on the earth."

EPHESIANS 6:1-3 NKJV

Tarry at the promise till God meets you there. He always returns by way of His promises.

L. B. COWMAN

I will bless you and make your name great, and
you will be a blessing.

GENESIS 12:2 NIV

Each day is a treasure box of gifts from God, just waiting
to be opened. Open your gifts with excitement. You will
find forgiveness attached to ribbons of joy. You will find
love wrapped in sparkling gems.

JOAN CLAYTON

Lift up your eyes.
Your heavenly Father waits to bless you—
in inconceivable ways to make your life
what you never dreamed it could be.

ANNE ORTLUND

I thank God, my mother,
for the blessing you are...
for the joy of your laughter...
the comfort of your prayers...
the warmth of your smile.

May the Lord, the God of your fathers, increase you
a thousand times and bless you as He has promised!

DEUTERONOMY 1:11 NIV

Bless our children, God, and help us
so to fashion their souls by precept and example
that they may ever love the good,
flee from sin, revere Thy Word,
and honor Thy name.

UNION PRAYER BOOK

God has not promised
sun without rain,
joy without sorrow,
peace without pain.
But God has promised
strength for the day,
rest for the labor,
light for the way,
grace for the trials,
help from above,
unfailing sympathy,
undying love.

ANNIE JOHNSON FLINT

I wish I had a box,
the biggest I could find,
I'd fill it right up to the brim
with everything that's kind.
A box without a lock, of course,
and never any key;
for everything inside that box
would then be offered free.
Grateful words for joys received
I'd freely give away.
Oh, let us open wide a box
of praise for every day.

The Gift
of Simplicity

The incredible gift of the ordinary!
Glory comes streaming from
the table of daily life.

MACRINA WIEDERKEHR

Happy people...enjoy the fundamental, often very simple things of life.... They savor the moment, glad to be alive, enjoying their work, their families, the good things around them. They are adaptable; they can bend with the wind, adjust to the changes in their times, enjoy the contest of life.... Their eyes are turned outward; they are aware, compassionate. They have the capacity to love.

JANE CANFIELD

My childhood home was the home of a woman with a genius for inventing daily life, who found happiness in the simplest of gestures.

LAURA FRONTY

Let us consider how we may spur one another on toward love and good deeds. Let us not give up meeting together, as some are in the habit of doing, but let us encourage one another.

HEBREWS 10:24-25 NIV

Enjoy the little things. One day you may look back and realize...they were the big things.

It doesn't take monumental feats to make the world a better place. It can be as simple as letting someone go ahead of you in a grocery line.

BARBARA JOHNSON

Not every day of our lives is overflowing with joy and celebration. But there are moments when our hearts nearly burst within us for the sheer joy of being alive. The first sight of our newborn babies, the warmth of love in another's eyes, the fresh scent of rain on a hot summer's eve—moments like these renew in us a heartfelt appreciation for life.

GWEN ELLIS

31

He guides the humble in what is right
and teaches them His way.

PSALM 25:9 NIV

*With our children who thrive on
simple pleasures, our work and
our entire society can be renewed.*

SARA WENGER SHENK

Don't ever let yourself get so busy that you miss those
little but important extras in life—the beauty of a day…
the smile of a friend…the serenity of a quiet
moment alone. For it is often life's smallest pleasures and
gentlest joys that make the biggest
and most lasting difference.

A fiery sunset, tiny pansies by the wayside, the sound of
raindrops tapping on the roof—what extraordinary
delight we find in the simple wonders of life!
With wide eyes and full hearts, we may cherish
what others often miss.

A devout life does bring wealth,
but it's the rich simplicity of being yourself
before God. Since we entered the world penniless
and will leave it penniless, if we have bread
on the table and shoes on our feet,
that's enough.

1 TIMOTHY 6:6 THE MESSAGE

It isn't the great big pleasures that count the most;
it's making a great deal out of the little ones.

JEAN WEBSTER

It is the little things that count
And give a mother pleasure—
The things her children bring to her
Which they so richly treasure...
The picture that is smudged a bit
With tiny fingerprints,
The colored rock, the lightning bugs,
The sticky peppermints;
The ragged, bright bouquet of flowers
A child brings, roots and all—
These things delight a mother's heart
Although they seem quite small.
A mother can see beauty
In the very smallest thing
For there's a little bit of heaven
In a small child's offering.

KATHERINE NELSON DAVIS

My Heart
Is Content

God bless you and utterly satisfy your heart...
with Himself.

Amy Carmichael

It is always wise to stop wishing for things long enough
to enjoy the fragrance of those now flowering.

PATRICE GIFFORD

Children have neither past nor future; they enjoy the present, which very few of us do.

JEAN DE LA BRUYÉRE

For I have learned in whatever state I am, to be content.
I know what it is to be in need, and I know what it is to
have plenty. I have learned the secret of being content
in any and every situation, whether well fed or hungry,
whether living in plenty or in want.

PHILIPPIANS 4:11-12 NKJV

Life is not intended to be simply a round of work,
no matter how interesting and important that work
may be. A moment's pause to watch the glory of a sunrise
or a sunset is soul satisfying, while a bird's song will set
the steps to music all day long.

LAURA INGALLS WILDER

My heart is content with just knowing
The treasures of life's little things;
The thrill of a child when it's snowing,
The trill of a bird in the spring.
My heart is content with just knowing
Fulfillment that true friendship brings;
It fills to the brim, overflowing
With pleasure in life's "little things."

JUNE MASTERS BACHER

If you're content to simply be yourself,
your life will count for plenty.

MATTHEW 23:11 THE MESSAGE

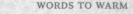
Where the soul is full of peace and joy,
outward surroundings and circumstances are of
comparatively little account.

HANNAH WHITALL SMITH

Women of adventure have conquered their fates and
know how to live exciting and fulfilling lives right where
they are. They have learned to reinvent themselves and
find creative ways to enjoy the world and their place in it.
They know how to take mini-vacations, stop and smell
the roses, and live fully in the moment.

BARBARA JENKINS

Let the day suffice, with all its joys and failings,
its little triumphs and defeats…. Happily, if sleepily,
welcome evening as a time of rest, and let it
slip away, losing nothing.

KATHLEEN NORRIS

When we put people before possessions in our hearts, we are sowing seeds of enduring satisfaction.

BEVERLY LaHAYE

I am still determined to be cheerful and happy,
in whatever situation I may be; for I have also learned
from experience that the greater part of our happiness or
misery depends upon our dispositions, and not upon
our circumstances.

MARTHA WASHINGTON

We brought nothing into the world, so we can take
nothing out. But, if we have food and clothes,
we will be satisfied with that.

1 TIMOTHY 6:7-8 NCV

God is helping me to be content to set certain gifts
on the shelf at present for the sake of my family.
He is teaching me that He is more interested
in what I am than in what I do.

SANDRA K. STRUBHAR

Normal day, let me be aware of the treasure you are.
Let me learn from you, love you, bless you before
you depart. Let me not pass you by in quest of some
rare and perfect tomorrow.

Everything has its wonders, even darkness and silence,
and I learn, whatever state I may be in,
therein to be content.

HELEN KELLER

Contentment is not the fulfillment of what you want,
but the realization of how much you already have.

Providing
All
Our Needs

Children will not remember you
for the material things you provided,
but for the feeling that you cherished them.

GAIL GRENIER SWEET

I must simply be thankful, and I am,
for all the Lord has provided for me,
whether big or small in the eyes of someone else.

MABEL P. ADAMSON

She is their earth....
She is their food and their bed
and the extra blanket when it grows cold in the night;
she is their warmth and their health
and their shelter.

KATHERINE BUTLER HATHAWAY

They might not need me;
but they might.
I'll let my head be just in sight;
A smile as small as mine might be
Precisely their necessity.

EMILY DICKINSON

You can trust God right now to supply all your needs
for today. And if your needs are more tomorrow,
His supply will be greater also.

*It is not my business to think
about myself. My business is to
think about God. It is for God
to think about me.*

SIMONE WEIL

It is the Lord who provides the sun to light the day
and the moon and stars to light the night,
and who stirs the sea into roaring waves.

JEREMIAH 31:35 NLT

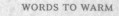
Provide me with the insight
that comes only from Your Word.

PSALM 119:169 THE MESSAGE

The very word "motherhood" has an emotional depth and
significance few terms have. It bespeaks nourishment and
safety and sheltering arms.

MARJORIE HOLMES

Those who know God as their Father know the
whole secret. They are His heirs, and may enter now into
possession of all that is necessary for their present needs.

HANNAH WHITALL SMITH

Throughout the Bible, when God asked someone
to do something, methods, means, materials and specific
directions were always provided. That person
had one thing to do: obey.

ELISABETH ELLIOT

You care for the land and water it;
You enrich it abundantly. The streams of God are
filled with water to provide the people with grain,
for so You have ordained it.

PSALM 65:9 NIV

God's gifts make us truly wealthy.
His loving supply never shall
leave us wanting.

BECKY LAIRD

There will be days which are great and everything goes
as planned. There will be other days when we aren't sure
why we got out of bed. Regardless of which kind of day it
is, we can be assured that God takes care of
our daily needs.

EMILIE BARNES

A mother is a person who, seeing there are only four pieces of pie for five people, promptly announces she never did care for pie.

TENNEVA JORDAN

If you have a special need today, focus your full attention on the goodness and greatness of your Father rather than on the size of your need. Your need is so small compared to His ability to meet it.

Tradition is a form of promise from parent to child. It's a way to say, "I love you," "I'm here for you," and "Some things will not change."

LYNN LUDWICK

Be
Encouraged

Whatever you do,
put romance and enthusiasm
into the lives of your children.

MARGARET R. MACDONALD

Encouragement is being a good listener, being positive,
letting others know you accept them for who they are.
It is offering hope, caring about the feelings of another,
understanding.

GIGI GRAHAM TCHIVIDJIAN

*Being taken for granted can be
a compliment. It means that
you've become a comfortable,
trusted person in another
person's life.*

JOYCE BROTHERS

For we have great joy and consolation in your love,
because the hearts of the saints have been
refreshed by you.

PHILEMON 1:7 NKJV

A word of encouragement to those we meet, a cheerful
smile in the supermarket, a card or letter to a friend,
a readiness to witness when opportunity is given—
all are practical ways in which we may let
His light shine through us.

ELIZABETH B. JONES

God, bless all young mothers at end of day.
Kneeling wearily with each small one to hear them pray.
Too tired to rise when done...and yet they do;
longing just to sleep one whole night through.
Too tired to sleep.... Too tired to pray....
God, bless all young mothers at close of day.

RUTH BELL GRAHAM

I wanted you to see what real courage is.... It's when you
know you're licked before you begin but you begin
anyway and you see it through no matter what.

HARPER LEE

A mother is someone who dreams great dreams for you,
but then she lets you chase the dreams you have for
yourself and loves you just the same. In the end,
she believes in your dreams as much as you do.

Hope begins in the dark, the stubborn hope that if you
just show up and try to do the right thing, the dawn
will come. You wait and watch and work:
You don't give up.

ANNE LAMOTT

I'm sure now I'll see God's goodness in the
exuberant earth. Stay with God! Take heart. Don't quit.

PSALM 27:13 THE MESSAGE

The stars exist that we might know how high
our dreams can soar.

Calm me, O Lord, as You stilled the storm,
Still me, O Lord, keep me from harm.
Let all the tumult within me cease,
Enfold me, Lord, in Your peace.

CELTIC TRADITIONAL

At night
I turn my problems over to God.
He's going to be
up all night anyway.

CARRIE WESTINGSON

The Scriptures give us hope and encouragement as we
wait patiently for God's promises to be fulfilled.

ROMANS 15:4 NLT

There are times when encouragement means such a lot.
And a word is enough to convey it.

GRACE STRICKER DAWSON

A mother is one who knows you as you really are,
understands where you've been,
accepts who you've become,
and still gently invites you to grow.

Some days, it is enough encouragement
just to watch the clouds break up and disappear,
leaving behind a blue patch of sky
and bright sunshine that is
so warm upon my face.
It's a glimpse of divinity;
a kiss from heaven.

Taking Time to Love

Dear Lord, please help me to remember
to take the time to bestow the kisses today
that I want loved ones
to remember tomorrow.

JENNIFER THOMAS

Be still, and in the quiet moments,
listen to the voice of your heavenly Father.
His words can renew your spirit...
no one knows you and your needs like He does.

JANET WEAVER SMITH

*Blessed is the person who is too busy
to worry in the daytime and too
sleepy to worry at night.*

CAROLINE SCHROEDER

Forgetting those things which are behind and reaching
forward to those things which are ahead, I press toward
the goal for the prize of the upward call of God
in Christ Jesus.

PHILIPPIANS 3:13-14 NKJV

Can you measure the worth of a sunbeam,
The worth of a treasured smile,
The value of love and of giving,
The things that make life worthwhile?...
Can you measure the value of friendship,
Of knowing that someone is there,
Of faith and of hope and of courage,
A treasured and goodly share?
For nothing is higher in value,
Whatever life chooses to send—
We must prove that we, too, are worthy
And equal the worth of a friend.

GARNETT ANN SCHULTZ

We must not, in trying to think about how we can make
a big difference, ignore the small daily differences we can
make which, over time, add up to big differences
that we often cannot foresee.

MARIAN WRIGHT EDELMAN

Make the most of every opportunity. Be gracious in your speech. The goal is to bring out the best in others.

COLOSSIANS 4:5 THE MESSAGE

Mama's order was heavenly. It had to do with thoroughness...and taking plenty of time. It had to do with taking plenty of time with me.

SUSANNAH LESSARD

Getting things accomplished isn't nearly as important as taking time for love.

JANETTE OKE

Live each day the fullest you can, not guaranteeing there'll be a tomorrow, not dwelling endlessly on yesterday.

JANE SEYMOUR

*Take time to notice all the usually
unnoticed, simple things in life.
Delight in the never-ending hope
that's available every day!*

Choices can change our lives profoundly.
The choice to mend a broken relationship,
to say yes to a difficult assignment,
to lay aside some important work to play with a child,
to visit some forgotten person—
these small choices may affect our lives eternally.

GLORIA GAITHER

Time is a very precious gift of God; so precious that it's
only given to us moment by moment.

AMELIA BARR

Just accept the fact that as long as you have children in
your home, your house is going to get messy.

LISA WHELCHEL

Generous people will be blessed, because they
share their food with the poor.

PROVERBS 22:9 NCV

See each morning a world made anew,
as if it were the morning of the very first day;...
treasure and use it,
as if it were the final hour
of the very last day.

FAY HARTZELL ARNOLD

True worth is in being, not seeming—
In doing, each day that goes by,
Some little good—not in dreaming
Of great things to do by and by.

ALICE CARY

I
Believe

Faith allows us to continually delight in life
since we have placed our needs in God's hands.
<small>Janet Weaver Smith</small>

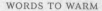
I believe in the sun even if it isn't shining.
I believe in love even when I am alone.
I believe in God even when He is silent.

*Faith sees the invisible,
believes the incredible,
and receives the impossible.*

Your mercy, O Lord, is in the heavens;
Your faithfulness reaches to the clouds.

PSALM 36:5 NKJV

Within each of us there is an inner place
where the living God Himself longs to dwell,
our sacred center of belief.

Faith is not an effort,
a striving, a ceaseless seeking,
as so many earnest souls suppose,
but rather a letting go,
an abandonment,
an abiding rest in God that nothing,
not even the soul's shortcomings,
can disturb.

I think miracles exist in part as gifts
and in part as clues that there is
something beyond the flat world we see.

Peggy Noonan

Be alert. Continue strong in the faith.
Have courage, and be strong.

1 Corinthians 16:13 NCV

If it can be verified, we don't need faith.... Faith is for
that which lies on the other side of reason. Faith is what
makes life bearable, with all its tragedies and ambiguities
and sudden, startling joys.

MADELEINE L'ENGLE

I pray that Christ will live in your hearts by faith and that
your life will be strong in love and be built on love.

EPHESIANS 3:17 NCV

Not everyone possesses boundless energy or a
conspicuous talent. We are not equally blessed with great
intellect or physical beauty or emotional strength.
But we have all been given the same ability to be faithful.

GIGI GRAHAM TCHIVIDJIAN

I see Heaven's glories shine,
And faith shines equal, arming me from fear.

EMILY BRONTË

*True faith drops its letter in the
post office box and lets it go.
Distrust holds on to a corner of it
and wonders that the answer
never comes.*

L. B. COWMAN

Faith expects from God what is
beyond all expectations.

Finding acceptance with joy, whatever
the circumstances of life—whether they are
petty annoyances or fiery trials—
this is a living faith that grows.

MARY LOU STEIGLEDER

Faith means
being sure of what we hope for...now.
It means knowing something is real,
this moment, all around you,
even when you don't see it.
Great faith isn't the ability to believe
long and far into the misty future.
It's simply taking God at His word
and taking the next step.

JONI EARECKSON TADA

A Covering
of Prayer

Loving Creator, help me reawaken
my childlike sense of wonder
at the delights of Your world!

MARILYN MORGAN HELLEBERG

When you were small
And just a touch away,
I covered you with blankets
Against the cool night air.
But now that you are tall
And out of reach,
I fold my hands
And cover you with prayer.

DONA MADDUX COOPER

When we call on God,
He bends down His ear to listen,
as a father bends down
to listen to his little child.

ELIZABETH CHARLES

We need quiet time to examine our lives openly and
honestly.... Spending quiet time alone gives your mind
an opportunity to renew itself and create order.

SUSAN L. TAYLOR

If a care is too small to be turned into a prayer
then it is too small to be made into a burden.

As soon as I pray, You answer me;
You encourage me by giving me strength.

PSALM 138:3 NLT

Lord, thank You for my children.
Please inspire me with ways to show them
my love and Yours.
I want them to feel appreciated.
I want to help and encourage them....
I want to bless them.

QUIN SHERRER

Open wide the windows of our spirits and fill us
full of light; open wide the door of our hearts that
we may receive and entertain Thee with all the
powers of our adoration.

CHRISTINA ROSSETTI

I said a prayer for you today
And I know God must have heard,
I felt the answer in my heart
Although He spoke no word.
I asked that He'd be near you
At the start of each new day,
To grant you health and blessings
And friends to share the way.
I asked for happiness for you
In all things great and small,
But it was His loving care
I prayed for most of all.

Always be joyful.
Pray continually, and give thanks
whatever happens. That is what God
wants for you in Christ Jesus.

1 THESSALONIANS 5:16-18 NCV

We must take our troubles to the Lord,
but we must do more than that;
we must leave them there.

HANNAH WHITALL SMITH

Whate'er the care which breaks thy rest,
Whate'er the wish that swells thy breast;
Spread before God that wish, that care,
And change anxiety to prayer.

You pay God a compliment by asking
great things of Him.

TERESA OF AVILA

Allow your dreams a place in your prayers and plans.
God-given dreams can help you move into the future
He is preparing for you.

BARBARA JOHNSON

Be kindly affectionate to one another,...
fervent in spirit, serving the Lord;
rejoicing in hope, patient in tribulation,
continuing steadfastly in prayer;
distributing to the needs of the saints,
given to hospitality.

ROMANS 12:10-12 NKJV

It is when things go wrong,
when good things do not happen,
when our prayers seem to have been lost,
that God is most present.

MADELEINE L'ENGLE

The Strength of Family

Family faces are magic mirrors.
Looking at people who belong to us,
we see the past, present, and future.

GAIL LUMET BUCKLEY

A Mother's love is something
that no one can explain,
It is made of deep devotion
and of sacrifice and pain....
It believes beyond believing
when the world around condemns,
And it glows with all the beauty
of the rarest, brightest gems.

HELEN STEINER RICE

As if that weren't enough,
You've blessed my family
so that it will continue
in Your presence always.
Because You have blessed it, God,
it's really blessed—
blessed for good!

1 CHRONICLES 17:16 THE MESSAGE

We were a strange little band of characters, trudging through life sharing diseases and toothpaste, coveting one another's desserts, hiding shampoo, borrowing money, locking each other out of our rooms, inflicting pain and kissing to heal it in the same instant, loving, laughing, defending, and trying to figure out the common thread that bound us all together.

ERMA BOMBECK

Call it clan, call it a network, call it a tribe, call it a family. Whatever you call it, whoever you are, you need one.

JANE HOWARD

Families give us many things—love and meaning, purpose and an opportunity to give, and a sense of humor.

I hope my children look back on today,
And see a mom who had time to play.
There will be years for cleaning and cooking,
For children grow up while we're not looking.

If there be one thing pure...
that can endure, when all else passes
away...it is a mother's love.

MARCHIONESS DE SPADARA

We really need only five things on this earth: Some food,
some sun, some work, some fun, and someone.

BEATRICE NOLAN

74

Sooner or later we all discover
that the important moments in life
are not the advertised ones,
not the birthdays, the graduations, the weddings,
not the great goals achieved.
The real milestones are less prepossessing.
They come to the door of memory.

SUSAN B. ANTHONY

As for me and my family, we will serve the Lord.

JOSHUA 24:15 NCV

The effect of having other interests
beyond those domestic works well.
The more one does and sees and feels,
the more one is able to do,
and the more genuine may be one's appreciation
of fundamental things like home,
and love, and understanding companionship.

AMELIA EARHART

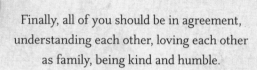

Finally, all of you should be in agreement,
understanding each other, loving each other
as family, being kind and humble.

1 Peter 3:8 ncv

Women know
The way to rear up children (to be just);
They know a simple, merry, tender knack
Of tying sashes, fitting baby-shoes,
And stringing pretty words that make no sense,
And kissing full sense into empty words;
Which things are corals to cut life upon,
Although such trifles.

Elizabeth Barrett Browning

Thank You, Lord!

Thank You, Father,
for loving all the little children
of the world—
no matter how old we are.
MARION BOND WEST

Morning has broken like the first morning,
Blackbird has spoken like the first bird....
Praise with elation, praise every morning,
God's re-creation of the new day!

ELEANOR FARJEON

Every day shared with the ones we love is a gift for which we are very thankful!

Mothers are lots of things—doctors, writers, lawyers, gardeners, actresses, cooks, police officers, sometimes even truck drivers. And mothers. Thank You, Lord.

MADELEINE L'ENGLE

Sing praises to the Lord, you who belong to Him;
praise His holy name.

PSALM 30:4 NCV

Then we, Your people, the ones You love and care for,
will thank You over and over and over.
We'll tell everyone we meet how wonderful You are,
how praiseworthy You are!

PSALM 79:13 THE MESSAGE

May your life become one of glad and unending praise to
the Lord as you journey through this world, and in the
world that is to come!

TERESA OF AVILA

God desires that the work we do bring us enduring joy
and satisfaction. This will naturally happen when our
efforts are labors of love that bring Him glory
and praise.

BEVERLY LAHAYE

They that trust the Lord find many things to praise
Him for. Praise follows trust.

LILY MAY GOULD

Our thanksgiving today should include those things which we take for granted, and we should continually praise our God, who is true to His promise, who has provided and retained the necessities for our living.

BETTY FUHRMAN

Let's praise His name! He is holy, He is almighty. He is love. He brings hope, forgiveness, heart cleansing, peace and power. He is our deliverer and coming King. Praise His wonderful name!

LUCILLE M. LAW

How much of our lives are...well...so daily. How often our hours are filled with the mundane, seemingly unimportant things that have to be done, whether at home or work. These very "daily" tasks could become a celebration of praise. "It is through consecration," someone has said, "that drudgery is made divine."

GIGI GRAHAM TCHIVIDJIAN

Thanksgiving puts power in living,
because it opens the generators of the heart
to respond gratefully,
to receive joyfully,
and to react creatively.

I have never committed the least matter to God, that I have not had reason for infinite praise.

ANNA SHIPTON

Thank God for dirty dishes;
They have a tale to tell.
While other folks go hungry,
We're eating pretty well.
With home, and health, and happiness,
We shouldn't want to fuss;
For by this stack of evidence,
God's very good to us.

81

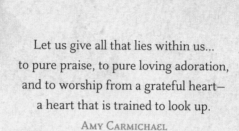

Let us give all that lies within us...
to pure praise, to pure loving adoration,
and to worship from a grateful heart—
a heart that is trained to look up.

AMY CARMICHAEL

God, of Your goodness give me Yourself,
for You are enough for me.
And only in You do I have everything.

JULIAN OF NORWICH

Let us continually offer the sacrifice of praise to God,
that is, the fruit of our lips, giving thanks to His name.
But do not forget to do good and to share,
for with such sacrifices God is well pleased.

HEBREWS 13:15-16 NKJV

The Richness of Friendship

We are so very rich
if we know just a few people
in a way in which we know no others.

CATHERINE BRAMWELL BOOTH

Knowing what to say is not always necessary;
just the presence of a caring friend
can make a world of difference.

SHERI CURRY

*Instant availability
without continuous presence
is probably the best role
a mother can play.*

L. BAILYN

Insomuch as any one pushes you nearer to God,
he or she is your friend.

FRENCH PROVERB

Friends love through all kinds of weather,
and families stick together in all kinds of trouble.

PROVERBS 17:17 NCV

If we would build on a sure foundation in friendship,
we must love friends for their sake
rather than for our own.

CHARLOTTE BRONTË

Oh, the comfort, the inexpressible comfort
of feeling *safe* with a person—having neither
to weigh thoughts nor measure words,
but pouring them all right out just as they are,
chaff and grain together, certain that
a faithful hand will take and sift them,
keep what is worth keeping and then,
with the breath of kindness,
blow the rest away.

DINAH MARIA MULOCK CRAIK

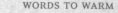

Stay true to the Lord.
I love you and long to see you, dear friends,
for you are my joy.

PHILIPPIANS 4:1 NLT

Don't walk in front of me—I may not follow.
Don't walk behind me—I may not lead.
Walk beside me—And just be my friend.

Having someone who understands
is a great blessing for ourselves.
Being someone who understands
is a great blessing to others.

JANETTE OKE

Friendship is the fruit gathered from the trees
planted in the rich soil of love, and nurtured
with tender care and understanding.

ALMA L. WEIXELBAUM

We should all have one person who knows how to bless us
despite the evidence.

PHYLLIS THEROUX

*Treat your friends like family
and your family like friends.*

Everyone was meant to share
God's all-abiding love and care;
He saw that we would need to know
a way to let these feelings show....
So God made hugs.

JILL WOLF

I am only as strong as the coffee I drink,
the hairspray I use, and the friends I have.

The Lord is a friend to those who fear Him.
He teaches them His covenant.

PSALM 25:14 NLT

Good communication is stimulating as black coffee,
and just as hard to sleep after.

ANNE MORROW LINDBERGH

A friend understands what you are trying to say...
even when your thoughts aren't fitting into words.

ANN D. PARRISH

A friend hears the song in my heart and sings it to me
when my memory fails.

Listening...means taking a vigorous, human interest in
what is being told us. You can listen like a blank wall
or like a splendid auditorium where every sound
comes back fuller and richer.

ALICE DUER MILLER

Love
All Around

No one ever outgrows
the need for a mother's love.

My mother and I have
laughed over nothing
and cried over everything.
We understand each other's fears,
losses, and sense of humor.
She holds my heart
like no one else can.

JANETTE OKE

*The human heart,
at whatever age,
opens only to the heart
that opens in return.*

MARIA EDGEWORTH

Only He who created
the wonders of the world
entwines hearts in an eternal way.

There is no need to plead
that the love of God shall fill our hearts
as though He were unwilling to fill us....
Love is pressing around us on all sides
like air. Cease to resist it and
instantly love takes possession.

AMY CARMICHAEL

You gave me life and
showed me Your unfailing love.
My life was preserved by Your care.

JOB 10:12 NLT

You have to love your children unselfishly.
That's hard.
But it's the only way.

BARBARA BUSH

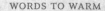

Love grows from our capacity to
give what is deepest within ourselves
and also receive what is the deepest
within another person.
The heart becomes an ocean strong and deep,
launching all on its tide.

Being a full-time mother is one of the highest-salaried
jobs in any field since the payment is pure love.

MILDRED B. VERMONT

Nothing can separate you from His love,
absolutely nothing....
God is enough for time,
and God is enough for eternity.
God is enough!

HANNAH WHITALL SMITH

Love the Lord God with all your passion and prayer
and intelligence and energy.

MARK 12:30 THE MESSAGE

To love by freely giving is its own reward.
To be possessed by love and to in turn give love away
is to find the secret of abundant life.

GLORIA GAITHER

*A mother's love is the heart of
the home. Her children's sense of
security and self-worth are
found there.*

God will never let you be shaken or moved
from your place near His heart.

JONI EARECKSON TADA

Open your hearts to the love God instills....
God loves you tenderly. What He gives you is not to be
kept under lock and key, but to be shared.

MOTHER TERESA

For You bless the godly, O Lord;
You surround them with Your shield of love.

PSALM 5:12 NLT

What we have once enjoyed we can never lose.
All that we love deeply becomes a part of us.

HELEN KELLER

Women can do no greater thing
than to create the climate of love in their homes.
Love which spoils and pampers,
weakens and hampers.
Real love strengthens and matures
and leaves the loved one free to grow.

EUGENIA PRICE

Special Gifts
We Share

It is a special gift
to be able to view the world
through the eyes of a child.

Oh God, You have given me...a life of clay.
Put Your big hands around mine and guide my hands
so that every time I make a mark on this life,
it will be Your mark.

GLORIA GAITHER

*God does not ask your ability or
your inability. He asks only
your availability.*

MARY KAY ASH

We should make the most of what God gives, both the
bounty and the capacity to enjoy it, accepting what's
given and delighting in the work. It's God's gift!
God deals out joy in the present, the now.

ECCLESIASTES 5:18 THE MESSAGE

· · · · · · · · · · · · · · · · · · · ·

Since you are like no other being
ever created since the beginning of time,
you are incomparable.

BRENDA UELAND

Heavenly Father, thank You for the unique personalities
that You have given to each and every child. Help me to
discover each talent and gift with which You have blessed
my children, and may I learn how to best cultivate each of
the blossoms You have planted within their souls. Amen.

KIM BOYCE

God gave me my gifts. I will do all I can
to show Him how grateful I am to Him.

GRACE LIVINGSTON HILL

You know how to give good gifts to your children.
How much more your heavenly Father will give good
things to those who ask Him!

MATTHEW 7:11 NCV

God's designs regarding you, and His methods of bringing
about these designs, are infinitely wise.

MADAME JEANNE GUYON

Maybe all I could do was mother.... And yet, why did I feel
so fulfilled when I bedded down three kids between
clean sheets? What if raising and instilling values in three
children and turning them into worthwhile human beings
would be the most important contribution
I ever made in my lifetime?

ERMA BOMBECK

Each one of us is God's special work of art. Through us,
He teaches and inspires, delights and encourages, informs
and uplifts all those who view our lives.

JONI EARECKSON TADA

Give, and it will be given to you. A good measure,
pressed down, shaken together and running over,
will be poured into your lap. For with the measure you
use, it will be measured to you.

LUKE 6:38 NIV

*Our greatest responsibility today
may be the unselfish sacrifice of our
time, talent, and love in the lives of
those little ones around us.*

SUSAN DOWNS

This is the real gift: you have been given the breath of
life, designed with a unique, one-of-a-kind soul that exists
forever—the way that you choose to live it doesn't change
the fact that you've been given the gift of being now
and forever. Priceless in value, you are handcrafted by
God, who has a personal design and plan for each of us.

Whatever job I perform—whether changing a diaper, closing a deal, teaching a class, or writing a book—when I meet legitimate needs, I am carrying on God's work.

KATHY PEEL

I'll show my children right from wrong,
encourage dreams and hope;
explain respect for others,
while teaching them to cope
with outside pressures, inside fears,
a world that's less than whole;
and through it all I'll nurture
my children's most precious soul!
Though oftentimes a struggle,
this job I'll never trade;
for in my hand tomorrow lives…
a future God has made.

To Live, Laugh, and Love

If they like it, it serves four;
otherwise, six.

Elsie Zussman

Whole-hearted, ready laughter heals, encourages, relaxes anyone within hearing distance. The laughter that springs from love makes wide the space around—gives room for the loved one to enter in.

EUGENIA PRICE

Laugh at yourself first before anyone else can.

ELSA MAXWELL

A cheerful look brings joy to the heart;
good news makes for good health.

PROVERBS 15:30 NLT

One of the great joys of motherhood is the happiness our children bring into our lives. Let's make the effort to experience the laughter of childhood with our children.

KIM BOYCE

People can be divided into three groups: Those who make things happen, those who watch things happen, and those who wonder what happened.

Now, as always, the most automated appliance in a household is the mother.

BEVERLY JONES

Sense of humor; God's great gift
causes spirits to uplift,
Helps to make our bodies mend;
lightens burdens; cheers a friend;
Tickles children; elders grin
at this warmth that glows within;
Surely in the great hereafter
heaven must be full of laughter!

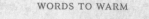

Take time to laugh. It is the music of the soul.

If you can learn to laugh in spite of the circumstances that surround you, you will enrich others, enrich yourself, and more than that, you will last!

BARBARA JOHNSON

A good day: When the wheels of your shopping cart all go in the same direction.

If it weren't for the last minute, nothing would get done.

May all who search for You
be filled with joy and gladness in You.

PSALM 40:16 NLT

Children seldom misquote you. They more often repeat
word for word what you shouldn't have said.

MAE MALOO

A good laugh is as good as a prayer sometimes.

LUCY MAUD MONTGOMERY

If you can remain calm, you just don't have all the facts.

Today's Forecast:
Partly rational with brief periods of coherent thought
giving way to complete apathy by tonight.

SHERRIE WEAVER

The surest way of having something done
is to forbid your kids to do it.

The best laughter, the laughter that can heal,
the laughter that has the truest ring, is the laughter that
flowers out of a love for life and its Giver.

MAXINE HANCOCK

In the world you will have tribulation; but be of
good cheer, I have overcome the world.

JOHN 16:33 NKJV

When children's eyes are smiling
'Tis God's love that's shining through
With glints of joy and laughter
What good medicine for you!

MARGARET FISHBACK POWERS

Blessed are they who can laugh at themselves, for they
shall never cease to be amused.

God
Our Father

If nothing seems to go my way today,
this is my happiness:
God is my Father and I am His child.

BASILEA SCHLINK

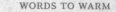

As a rose fills a room with its fragrance,
so will God's love fill our lives.

MARGARET BROWNLEY

God is every moment totally aware of each one of us.
Totally aware in intense concentration and love....
No one passes through any area of life, happy or tragic,
without the attention of God.

EUGENIA PRICE

For my dear little child I'd lasso the moon
and give you my love on a silver spoon.
I'd run 'round the world and back again, too,
to grant you the hope of days bright and new.
But all that I have and all that I do
is nothing compared to God's love for you.

Whoever walks toward God one step,
God runs toward him two.

JEWISH PROVERB

Blessed be the God and Father of our Lord Jesus Christ, the Father of mercies and God of all comfort, who comforts us in all our tribulation, that we may be able to comfort those who are in any trouble, with the comfort with which we ourselves are comforted by God.

2 CORINTHIANS 1:3-4 NKJV

After the love of God,
a mother's affection
is the greatest treasure
here below.

Children of the heavenly Father
Safely in His bosom gather;
Nestling bird nor star in heaven
Such a refuge e'er was given.

CAROLINA SANDELL BERG

Grace and peace to you from God our Father and
from the Lord Jesus Christ.

ROMANS 1:7 NIV

The treasure our heart searches for is found in the ocean of God's love.

JANET WEAVER SMITH

Before anything else, above all else,
beyond everything else, God loves us.
God loves us extravagantly,
ridiculously, without limit or condition.
God is in love with us...
God yearns for us.

ROBERTA BONDI

Blue skies with white clouds on summer days. A myriad of stars on clear moonlit nights. Tulips and roses and violets and dandelions and daisies. Bluebirds and laughter and sunshine and Easter. See how He loves us!

ALICE CHAPIN

The God who created, names, and numbers the stars in the heavens also numbers the hairs of my head.... He pays attention to very big things and to very small ones. What matters to me matters to Him, and that changes my life.

ELISABETH ELLIOT

How great is the love the Father has lavished on us, that we should be called children of God! And that is what we are! The reason the world does not know us is that it did not know Him.

1 JOHN 3:1 NIV

God walks with us.... He scoops us up in His arms or
simply sits with us in silent strength until we cannot
avoid the awesome recognition that yes,
even now, He is here.

GLORIA GAITHER

The Creator thinks enough of you to have sent
Someone very special so that you might have life—
abundantly, joyfully, completely, and victoriously.

God is so big He can cover the whole world with His love,
and so small He can curl up inside your heart.

JUNE MASTERS BACHER

Stand outside this evening. Look at the stars. Know that
you are special and loved by the One who created them.

Heart
Full of
Joy

An effort made for the happiness of others
lifts us above ourselves.

LYDIA MARIA CHILD

How necessary it is to cultivate a spirit of joy. It is
a psychological truth that the physical acts of reverence
and devotion make one feel devout. The courteous gesture
increases one's respect for others. To act lovingly is to
begin to feel loving, and certainly to act joyfully brings joy
to others which in turn makes one feel joyful. I believe we
are called to the duty of delight.

DOROTHY DAY

Sometimes the laughter in mothering is the recognition
of the ironies and absurdities. Sometime, though, it's just
pure, unthinking delight.

BARBARA SCHAPIRO

The Lord has filled my heart with joy; I feel very strong
in the Lord.... I am glad because You have helped me!

1 SAMUEL 2:1 NCV

Our hearts were made for joy. Our hearts
were made to enjoy the One who created them.
Too deeply planted to be much affected by
the ups and downs of life, this joy is a
knowing and a being known by our Creator.
He sets our hearts alight
with radiant joy.

*Joy is warm and radiant and
clamors for expressions
and experience.*

DOROTHY SEGOVIA

If one is joyful, it means that one is faithfully living
for God, and that nothing else counts;
and if one gives joy to others one is doing God's work.
With joy without and joy within, all is well.

JANET ERSKINE STUART

If a child is to keep his inborn sense of wonder...he needs
the companionship of at least one adult who can share it,
rediscovering with him the joy, excitement,
and mystery of the world we live in.

RACHEL CARSON

To be able to find joy in another's joy,
that is the secret of happiness.

All who seek the Lord will praise Him.
Their hearts will rejoice with everlasting joy.

PSALM 22:26 NLT

My hope for you today:
A double helping of laughter,
A cup full of love,
A heart brimming with joy!

When hands reach out in friendship,
hearts are touched with joy.

Joy is the feeling of grinning on the inside.

MELBA COLGROVE

God knows everything about us.
And He cares about everything.
Moreover, He can manage every situation.
And He loves us! Surely this is enough
to open the wellsprings of joy....
And joy is always a source of strength.

HANNAH WHITALL SMITH

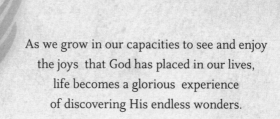

As we grow in our capacities to see and enjoy
the joys that God has placed in our lives,
life becomes a glorious experience
of discovering His endless wonders.

The Lord is my strength and my shield;
my heart trusts in Him, and I am helped.
My heart leaps for joy and I will
give thanks to Him in song.

<small>Psalm 28:7 niv</small>

Since you get more joy
out of giving joy to others,
you should put a good deal
of thought into the happiness
that you are able to give.

<small>Eleanor Roosevelt</small>

A Mother's Influence

A mother is not a person to lean on,
but a person to make leaning unnecessary.

DOROTHY CANFIELD FISHER

The fullness of our heart is expressed in our eyes, in our touch, in what we write, in what we say, in the way we walk, the way we receive, the way we need.

MOTHER TERESA

The best thing that you can give your children, next to good habits, is good memories.

BARBARA JOHNSON

How blessed the man You train, God,
the woman You instruct in Your Word,
providing a circle of quiet within the clamor of evil....
God will never walk away from His people,
never desert His precious people.
Rest assured that justice is on its way
and every good heart put right.

PSALM 94:12-15 THE MESSAGE

God, help me to be honest so my children
will learn honesty.
Help me to be kind so my children
will learn kindness.
Help me to be faithful so my children
will learn faith.
Help me to love so that my children
will be loving.

MARIAN WRIGHT EDELMAN

Train up a child in the way he should go,
and when he is old he will not depart from it.

PROVERBS 22:6 NKJV

What we feel, think, and do this moment influences both
our present and the future in ways we may never know.
Begin. Start right where you are. Consider your
possibilities and find inspiration...to add more
meaning and zest to your life.

ALEXANDRA STODDARD

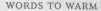
*There is no influence
so powerful as
that of the mother.*

SARAH JOSEPHA HALE

The blossom cannot tell
what becomes of its fragrance
as it drifts away,
just as no person can tell
what becomes of her influence
as she continues through life.

If our kids are going to make an impact in the world,
they must understand God's Word.

LISA WHELCHEL

Whether we are poets
or parents or teachers
or artists or gardeners,
we must start where we are
and use what we have.
In the process of
creation and relationship,
what seems mundane and trivial
may show itself to be
holy, precious, part of a pattern.

LUCI SHAW

To discipline a child produces wisdom.... Discipline your
children, and they will give you peace of mind
and will make your heart glad.

PROVERBS 29: 15, 17 NLT

Kindness is the only service
that will stand the storm of life
and not wash out.
It will wear well and be remembered
long after the prism of politeness
or the complexion of courtesy
has faded away.

The most important thing
she'd learned over the years
was that there was no way to be
a perfect mother and a million ways
to be a good one.

Jill Churchill

Gratitude

Happiness is a quiet,
perpetual rejoicing in small events.

Most of the people I know who have what I want—
which is to say, purpose, heart, balance, gratitude, joy—
are people with a deep sense of spirituality…. They are
part of something beautiful.

ANNE LAMOTT

Gratitude is the memory of the heart;
therefore forget not to say often,
I have all I ever enjoyed.

LYDIA MARIA CHILD

Let the peace of Christ rule in your hearts, since as
members of one body you were called to peace. And be
thankful. Let the word of Christ dwell in you richly as you
teach and admonish one another with all wisdom,
and as you sing psalms, hymns and spiritual songs with
gratitude in your hearts to God.

COLOSSIANS 3:15-16 NIV

We should look
for reasons to celebrate—
an A on a paper—
even a good hair day.

PAM FARREL

*That I am here is a
wonderful mystery to which
I will respond with joy.*

Feeling grateful or appreciative of someone or something
in your life actually attracts more of the things that you
appreciate and value into your life. And, the more of your
life that you like and appreciate, the healthier you'll be.

CHRISTIANE NORTHRUP

Experience God in the breathless wonder and startling beauty that is all around you. His sun shines warm upon your face. His wind whispers in the treetops. Like the first rays of morning light, celebrate the start of each day with God.

I will give You thanks, for You answered me; You have become my salvation.

PSALM 118:21 NIV

Were there no God we would be in this glorious world with grateful hearts and no one to thank.

CHRISTINA ROSSETTI

Gratitude unlocks the fullness of life. It turns what we have into enough, and more.... It can turn a meal into a feast, a house into a home, a stranger into a friend. Gratitude makes sense of our past, brings peace for today, and creates a vision for tomorrow.

MELODY BEATTIE